CARLSBAD CAVERNS

NATIONAL PARK

Silent Chambers, Timeless Beauty

by
John Barnett

CARLSBAD CAVERNS • GUADALUPE MOUNTAINS ASSOCIATION
Carlsbad, New Mexico

INTRODUCTION

The desert is subtle. Its gray-green miles pass slowly in seeming sameness; but hidden away in arroyos "out there" is the delicate beauty of a blossom nestled among the tangled thorns of a strawberry cactus, and the sight of a vermillion flycatcher knifing quickly into the air to catch a meal. For those who look closely the desert is a mixture of surprises great and small, almost never what it seemed at first.

Near Carlsbad, New Mexico is one of the great surprises. It is a cavern. To the casual visitor its dark entrance can be somewhat like one of the outworn images of the desert itself: unknown, perhaps uninteresting, maybe even a little bit ominous. Not so! Here again are subtlety and grandeur, where tiny drops of water, silently in the dark, can build a startlingly beautiful monument forty feet (12 m.) high. The desert's lower story is as unexpected as its surface, when finally one sees it.

There is one more wonder here, hidden more deeply than unexpected desert flowers, beyond even the stone astonishments of Carlsbad Cavern. Hidden by time itself is the story of how these other wonders came to be. Gradually we are piecing it together, and it turns out to involve unimaginable lengths of time, an ancient ocean with fish swimming where cactus are today, uplift of the very mountains, and the slow adaptation of life to new conditions.

It was Einstein who coined the phrase, "subtle, but not malicious"; he was talking about God but he could have meant the desert.

2

3

1. Natural Entrance to Carlsbad Cavern. Except for the trail, the awesome entrance to the cave has not been altered or enlarged in any manner. *George H. H. Huey*
2. Slaughter Canyon. The surface features at Carlsbad Caverns National Park are too often overlooked.
3. Visitor Center, Carlsbad Caverns National Park.

THE DESERT REVEALED

The surface around Carlsbad Cavern is a desert setting. With the park's primary attraction being the cavern itself, the abundance of beauty found on or near the rocky hills of the surface is often overlooked.

The cavern area is located in the northern part of the Chihuahuan Desert, most of which is in Mexico. The land is often barren looking — rolling dunes or flat desert clay spotted with creosote bush, mesquite, prickly pear or lechuguilla. One can see a desert sunrise that seems to burst into day; feel the gentle breezes that rustle leaves of trees sheltered in rocky canyons; marvel at thunderstorms that explode with little warning, creating instant rivers that disappear as quickly as they come; observe the struggle for existence among the wildlife; or savor a sunset that silhouettes a tall yucca against a painted sky. Each of these are isolated impressions of the desert; all of these, and many more, must be experienced to comprehend or get a "feel" for the desert.

There are nature trails and roadside exhibits in several places along the roadway to and from Carlsbad Cavern and also near the cavern entrance. These facilities provide beautiful and interesting views of the local topography and provide looks at the more common plant life of the region. Each is well worth a visit.

There is a great variety of plants in the Carlsbad area. Among the more common found on the rocky hills is lechuguilla. This plant is an agave and is one of the plants the Indians referred to as "mescal." Lechuguilla

is one of the indicator plants of the Chihuahuan Desert, being found nowhere else. It is about a foot (30 cm.) high with sharp pointed, slightly curved leaves. Like other agave plants, the lechuguilla lives for a number of years, finally grows a single tall stalk and blooms, and then dies. It often covers large areas and its sharp tips can make hiking or riding in the hills a hazardous adventure.

The Parry agave is also found in the area but is limited to higher elevations of the park. Usually known as the century plant, it is much more massive than lechuguilla. The bloom is one of the more spectacular found in the desert. The stalk can reach heights of 10 to 12 feet (3m. +) and the red and yellow blossoms occur in large clusters near the top.

Prickly pear occurs in great abundance. The large flat lobes are among the best known design of any desert plant. A variety of species is present — some with large stickers, others with tiny almost invisible thorns. Some have yellow blossoms, some orange. One species has large purple fruit that matures late in the summer after the blossoms have fallen away. These provide excellent food for both animal and human. Jams and jellies made from these "pears" are often among the favorites of southwestern desert dwellers.

Another cactus that is common is the cholla, or walking stick, an apt description. This plant has a woody skeleton beneath its fleshy exterior. When a stalk is dried out and stripped of the outside material, this skeleton has an unusual appearance and is often used to make curios characteristic of the Southwest.

Smaller cacti that are observed near Carlsbad include the strawberry cactus that has brilliant pink blossoms in the spring, the hedgehog cactus with bright red flowers, and

2

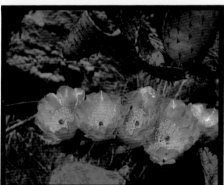

3

4

1. The Horseshoe Bend, Walnut Canyon. *George H. H. Huey*
2. Prickly pear cactus. *Hiram Parent*
3. Englemann prickly pear cactus
4. Claret cup cactus.
5. Pincushion cactus
6. Strawberry cactus

5

6

4

the pincushion or fishhook cactus.

Although the ocotillo is not a member of the cactus family, it is one of the thorniest and most unusual plants and covers many of the hillsides. It is the sole member of the candlewood family native to the United States. An ocotillo plant is a cluster of whiplike stalks that can reach heights of 10 feet (3 m.) or more. This plant has adapted to the desert life very well. In dry spells it drops its leaves; however, after a rainy period it is only a matter of days until tiny leaves cover the stalks. When the spike of red blossoms covers the tips of the stalks, it adds brilliant color to the rocky cliffs.

There are few trees that occur in the area and the ones that do are usually small and not widespread. Probably the most notable is the desert willow which is thickly laden with delicate white to lavender orchid-like blossoms when it blooms in summer. It is inconspicuous when not in bloom, but a great attraction when it is.

Mesquite, acacia, saltbush and creosote bush are common shrubs in the desert.

Wildlife, although not easily seen, is abundant in the caverns region. Mule deer are numerous; however they generally stay away from the more developed areas of the park during daylight hours. They are often seen near the roadway at night.

Coyotes, foxes, skunks, raccoons, and ringtails are fairly common in the park but rarely seen by visitors. They are generally nocturnal and roam the area when visitors are not present. Rabbits and squirrels are often seen during the day along roadways and near the cavern entrance.

Bird life is abundant and includes a large number of species ranging from hummingbirds to eagles. A checklist of birds observed within the boundaries of Carlsbad

2

3

4

Caverns National Park includes about 300 species. Among the more common are the black-throated sparrow, the rock wren, and the Say's phoebe. The uncommon cave swallow is found here nesting in the mouth of the cavern. The nighthawk is a summer resident and puts on a display of aerial acrobatics each summer evening. The turkey vulture soaring in lazy arcs through the summer sky does its job of clearing the carrion. Higher still, hawks and golden eagles range over the region and keep a sharp eye for prey.

Probably the most asked about creature is the rattlesnake. It is present, but seldom seen. Diamondback rattlers can be up to 6 feet (1.8 m.) in length and almost a foot (30 cm.) in circumference, so, to put it mildly, they can be imposing. Rattlers are not aggressive creatures — they use their poison to immobilize their prey; however, most other animals give the snakes a wide berth.

Lizards are often seen darting from place to place, only to stop, look around and then sprint on again. Most of the lizards blend into their surroundings remarkably well.

Scorpions, tarantulas, and centipedes are common throughout the area, along with countless varieties of insects.

The desert is not barren; it is unexpectedly full of life, both plants and animals. But that life has adapted to sparse conditions, and does not advertise itself to the casual eye.

5

1. Winter scenes like this occur infrequently and never last long. *Ron Kerbo*
2. Vermillion flycatcher
3. Kangaroo rat
4. Rock squirrel. *Hiram Parent*
5. Chihuahuan Desert after a summer thunderstorm
6. Mule deer

6

ANCIENT REFLECTIONS

Water, from oceans to tiny droplets, has created and shaped Carlsbad Cavern. The rocks in which the cavern formed are the product of an ancient reef that flourished 250 million years ago during the Permian period. The water was warm, and near the shore was a favorable place for a host of marine lime secreting plants and animals to live.

Generation followed generation and limy remains of the plants and animals, along with lime (calcium carbonate) that precipitated from the water, built up a reef along the edge of the inland sea. For millions of years as the entire region subsided, the reef grew upward and outward, maintaining a height just below sea level. Eventually the reef was hundreds of feet thick and one to four miles across. Behind the reef, on the tidal flats and in the lagoon behind them, limestone and occasional sandstone sheets were deposited at about the same rate the reef was growing. On the seaward side,

chunks of limestone broke away and tumbled down from the steep seaward face of the growing reef. These broken pieces of rock formed an underwater talus slope or rubble pile. The upper level of Carlsbad Cavern is in the thin layered back reef and tidal flat deposits, while the large chambers and lower levels are in the reef and reef talus deposits.

Eventually the channels supplying water from the ocean slowly closed, and the sea began to dry up. The water evaporated more rapidly than it was replaced. Salts and gypsum were precipitated and filled the basin. In time the basin was no more — the

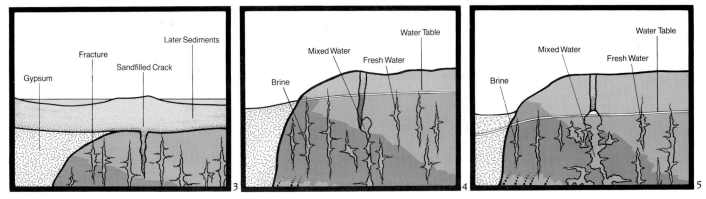

landscape was a nearly flat surface, with little relief. As eons passed, the old sea basin, the reef, and the surrounding regions were deeply buried under additional thousands of feet of sediments.

Starting with its burial and continuing as movement began to occur in more recent times, fractures developed in the old reef and overlying deposits.

As the Guadalupe Mountains were first raised by compressive earth movements (20-40 million years ago), fresh water filled some of the fractures. Fresh ground water mixed with briney waters saturating the basin-filling rocks, increasing the solubility of limestones. Sulfurous gasses, seeping upwards from far below and present in the brines, were oxidized to sulfuric acid and contributed to the processes of limestone dissolution.

Slowly — ever so slowly — these processes dissolved the adjacent limestone. Slow movements of the water carried the dissolved material away. This process of dissolving and removing continued over extreme lengths of time. The eventual result was a honeycomb of openings filled with water. The largest chambers in the cave occur at three levels (200, 750 and 830 feet) (60 m., 225 m., and 250 m.) below the present surface. Probably the water table remained static at these levels, so more time was available for dissolving the limestone.

Finally, 2-4 million years ago, massive earth movements again uplifted and tilted the entire region with the higher area to the west. Erosion stripped away the overlying sediments. The limestone of the exposed fossil reef was much harder than the basin salts and gypsum. Therefore, the old reef was much more resistant to erosion, and today the edge of the old sea basin is well marked

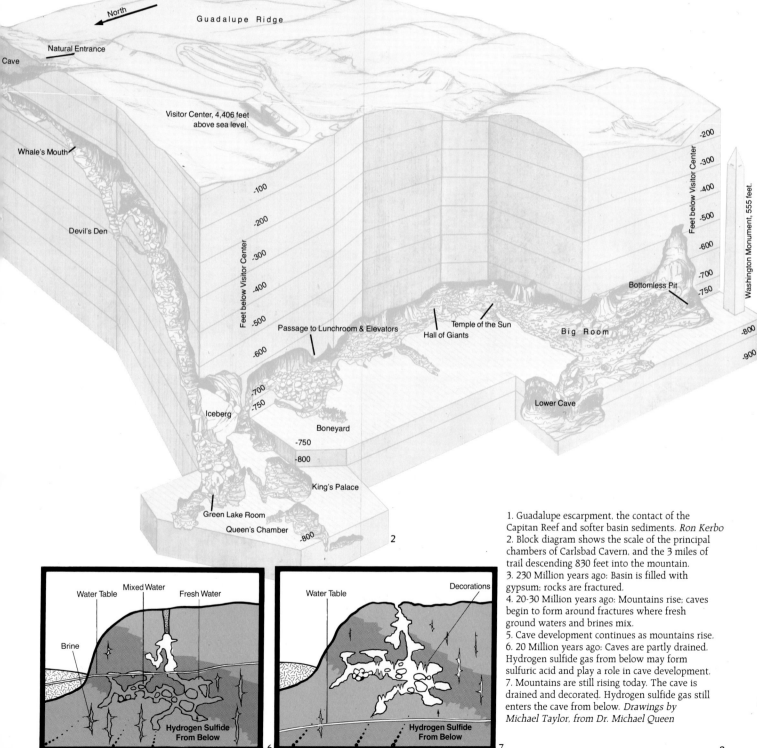

1. Guadalupe escarpment, the contact of the Capitan Reef and softer basin sediments. *Ron Kerbo*
2. Block diagram shows the scale of the principal chambers of Carlsbad Cavern, and the 3 miles of trail descending 830 feet into the mountain.
3. 230 Million years ago: Basin is filled with gypsum; rocks are fractured.
4. 20-30 Million years ago: Mountains rise; caves begin to form around fractures where fresh ground waters and brines mix.
5. Cave development continues as mountains rise.
6. 20 Million years ago: Caves are partly drained. Hydrogen sulfide gas from below may form sulfuric acid and play a role in cave development.
7. Mountains are still rising today. The cave is drained and decorated. Hydrogen sulfide gas still enters the cave from below. *Drawings by Michael Taylor, from Dr. Michael Queen*

by the ridge that extends from near the city of Carlsbad southwestward to Guadalupe Peak.

As uplift continued, ground water drained away leaving air-filled openings. With the loss of bouyancy that the ground water had supplied, many massive chunks of weakened rock could not support their own weight and collapse was commonplace, thus leaving large underground chambers and passageways. The basic shape of the cavern was fairly well defined by this time.

Massive deposits of gypsum are present in several locations in Carlsbad Cavern. While it is believed that the gypsum was brought into the cavern in solution, it is not yet clear just how or when the material was deposited.

Decoration of the cave began as chambers became air-filled. Even when lower parts of a chamber were still flooded, decoration began in the drained upper portions. Again, water is nature's primary tool in this process which is still going on. Rain and snow water percolating through the soil picks up a small amount of carbon dioxide from organic material and becomes a weak acid. Each drop can dissolve a tiny bit of limestone and carry it along on its downward trip. When the droplet reaches the air-filled chamber some carbon dioxide escapes into the cave air and the water's ability to hold limestone in solution is reduced. A tiny part of the limestone which was carried in is then precipitated from the water and left on the ceiling, wall, or floor of the chamber again as limestone or as calcite crystals. Drop after drop, depositing particle after particle — the cavern decorations are created.

Even though water has been the instrument of creation and decoration in Carlsbad Cavern, there is no evidence that any major flowing streams contributed to its

1. Aragonite crystals are chemically the same as calcite crystals but grow in different patterns. The crystals form when manganese, present in solution, acts as a catalyst resulting in beautiful, delicate formations.
2. Soda straws and helictites
3. Lake of the Clouds, Carlsbad Cavern. At 1037 feet (316 m.), Lake of the Clouds marks the deepest point below the cave entrance. The lake is 11 feet (3 m.) deep.

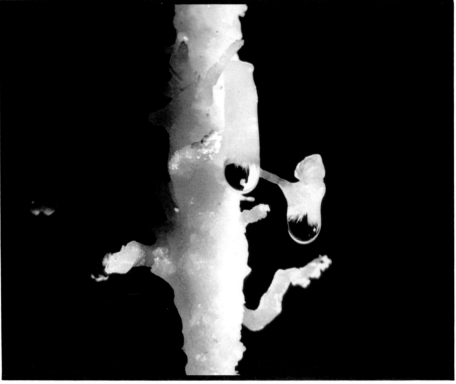

formation, although some minor streams may have followed a few passageways. There are areas where ponds have formed and stood for long periods of time. Some still exist today but they are very small. Green Lake, Mirror Lake and others are just a few feet across. Among the larger cavern pools is Lake of the Clouds which lies at the lowest known point in Carlsbad Cavern. Lake of the Clouds is located nearly ½ mile (.8 km.) away from the nearest public trail and at the bottom of a very steep-sided pit. The surface elevation of this small lake is over 1000 feet (300 m.) below the natural entrance. It is 11 feet (3 m.) deep, has no apparent drainage, and its level remains nearly constant.

We have no way of telling the exact age of any formation. The rate of growth depends on several variables such as water supply, rate of flow, amount of material carried, and other factors that can change drastically from place to place as well as from time to time.

PIERCING THE DARKNESS

Imagine the feelings of an early day Indian wanderer as he first viewed the black hole that later became known as Carlsbad Cavern. Whether it happened several thousand years ago, or only a few hundred, it must have been an awesome experience, especially if he was standing nearby as millions of bats spiraled their way skyward for an evening feeding.

It is very doubtful than any Indians ever went very far into the cave due to lack of light and the hazardous drop-off near the cave entrance. Indians did know of the cave; there are pictographs on the entrance walls and mescal cooking pits nearby, and bits of sandals have been found below the first big drop-off into the cave.

Although Indians apparently did not venture far into the cavern, the Apaches were masters of the rugged limestone mountains and used other caves in the Guadalupes for shelter. Despite many years of early Spanish exploration in the Southwest, no evidence has been found to indicate the Spanish explorers ever penetrated the Guadalupes, much less knew or cared about the many caverns that exist here.

The first people, other than the Indians, to cross the region were possibly gold seekers headed west, or military men, or map makers. The old Butterfield stage line ran just below the Guadalupe Ridge for a year. Still, exploration of Carlsbad Cavern had to wait until the West was tamed, political lines were drawn, Indian wars were settled, and ranching had finally begun.

We do not even know the name of the first cowboy who came upon the "mysterious" opening, or why he came, but it was in the late 1800s. Early reports state that in 1883 a twelve-year-old boy named Rolth Sublett was lowered into the cave by his father. His exploration was apparently limited to that part immediately below the entrance where natural light was available.

Two years later, a young man named Ned Shattuck and his father were searching for a stray cow and witnessed an evening bat flight from the cavern. They reported that the flight looked and sounded like a whirlwind.

Through such encounters, knowledge of the existence of a large cave containing countless numbers of bats slowly spread. Then economic minds began to churn. Where there were millions of bats there would be great deposits of guano, a nitrate rich fertilizer and a valuable commodity. In 1903 Abijah Long filed a claim for guano and other minerals on 40 acres (16 hectares) surrounding the mouth of what he called "Big Cave." Mining operations started soon thereafter. Mine cars were used to transport guano to the entrance. Then shafts were dug nearer to the vast deposits. Evidence of this

activity is still visible today. One of the mine cars is on display in the visitor center.

Most of the guano was shipped to southern California to help a developing citrus industry. In about 20 years of operation, over 100,000 tons of guano were taken from Carlsbad Cavern, amounting to about 90% of that in place when operations started. Six companies tried their hand at making it a financial success, but all failed due largely to high transportation costs.

As mining began, large numbers of people entered the cave; yet few of the miners explored more than the area near the

2

3

4

1. Soda straw forest, Guadalupe Room, Carlsbad Cavern
2. Scene from 1929 movie, "The Medicine Man." Filmed in Carlsbad Caverns, this scene depicts what early cave explorers must have gone through. Photo courtesy of Robert Nymeyer "Carlsbad, Caves, and a Camera," © 1978.
3. One of the many Indian midden circles or cooking pits found throughout the area
4. Pottery sherd found in Carlsbad Caverns National Park

entrance. The notable exception was James Larkin White. At one time or another Jim White worked for all but one of the guano mining companies. In his spare time he took his miner's lantern and probed deeper into the darkness, coming back with "wild" stories of what he had seen. Soon he convinced friends to go with him and see the wonders so long hidden from the world. Stories of the splendors slowly spread.

In 1922 the stories attracted the attention of Commissioner William Spry of the General Land Office. He initiated an investigation to determine if the cave was worthy of being set aside as a national monument. The man assigned to the investigation was Mineral Examiner Robert A. Holley, and his report was glowing. He wrote the following as an opening to his report:

"I enter upon this task with a feeling of temerity as I am wholly conscious of the feebleness of my efforts to convey in words the deep conflicting emotions, the feeling of fear and awe, and the desire for an inspired understanding of the Divine Creator's work that presents to the human eye such a complex aggregate of natural wonders in such a limited space."

Major Richard Burgess of El Paso was instrumental in having a geologist, Dr. Willis T. Lee, visit the cave. Dr. Lee's immediate recommendation, like Holley's, was in favor of a national monument. On October 25, 1923 President Calvin Coolidge signed a proclamation creating Carlsbad Cave National Monument.

The earliest visitors entered the cavern by standing in a large bucket that was lowered by cable down one of the mine shafts. Only two people could ride the bucket elevator on each 170 foot (51 m.) trip. Trails were constructed in the mid-1920s and made the

1. Visitors entering cavern, early 1920s
2. Jim White, an early explorer
3. The "Golden Stairs." This stairway is made of sacks of guano built over difficult portions of the trail.
4. Early visitors
5. Ladder leading to lower cave
6. Early visitors leaving the cavern in the "bucket elevator"

13

entry less "thrilling."

In the January 1924 edition of National Geographic Magazine, pictures by pioneer photographer Ray V. Davis and Dr. Lee were published with Dr. Lee's story of his party's explorations. The underground wonders were so unusual that when one of Mr. Davis' pictures was accidentally published upside down only a few people caught the error. Worldwide interest created then has continued to the present. National park status was obtained on May 14, 1930, when President Herbert Hoover signed into law a bill establishing Carlsbad Caverns National Park.

Today the visitor center stands near the cavern entrance. Paved trails lead the way down over the precipices and through the maze of rocks, and electric lights eliminate the need for torches. Still, every visitor who comes to Carlsbad Cavern surely feels a touch of the same sense of mystery and excitement that must have gone through the mind of each of those, who in his own time "discovered" Carlsbad Cavern — and that is as it should be.

VARIETY OF WONDERS

The variety of formations seems to be unending. Of the decorative formations, technically known as "speleothems," those most commonly known are stalactites and stalagmites. Stalactites hang from the ceiling and stalagmites grow upward from the floor. Park rangers often help visitors remember the difference by pointing out that stalactites hang "tite" to the ceiling and stalagmites "mite" reach the ceiling if they grow enough.

Stalactites begin with a drop of water that leaves a little ring of limestone on the ceiling. One after another, succeeding drops leave a little more limestone on that ring and a "soda straw" develops. A soda straw is a thin hollow tube through which more drops can move and deposit a little more limestone and further extend the tube. Some soda straws grow to lengths of several feet and yet remain less than a half-inch in diameter. If the tube becomes plugged, water moves outside the tube and the stalactite will take on an icicle-like shape.

When the water flow is fast enough, some drops fall to the floor. When deposition occurs there, the limestone deposited will grow upward. Stalagmites are usually much more massive than stalactites since the falling water tends to splatter over a larger area. They are usually rounded on top and have a proportionately thicker diameter. By far the largest cave formations found in Carlsbad Cavern are stalagmites. In the Hall of Giants several stalagmites reach heights of over 60 feet (18 m.) and have diameters over 10 feet (3 m.) and even then they are standing on a

2

3

4

5

6

1. Temple of the Sun, Big Room
2. Giant and Twin Domes
3. Whale's Mouth. Draperies are often called "cave bacon" and form only on sloping ceilings.
4. Lion's Tail, Big Room. The tip of the Lion's Tail marks an old water level in the Big Room.
5. Cave pearls. Cave pearls grow in individual cups in much the same manner as pearls from an oyster. They are sometimes as large as golf balls.
6. Draperies, Dome Room

massive limestone buildup.

Often a stalagmite will grow directly beneath a stalactite if they both are supplied from a single water source. When they grow enough to connect, they become a single formation that is referred to simply as a column. The Giant Dome in the Big Room and the Veiled Statue in the Green Lake Room are two of the more beautiful columns in Carlsbad Cavern.

Sloping ceilings often cause water to flow downward in peculiar fashions. The resulting limestone deposition can have a drapery effect, looking like a piece of cloth hung from the ceiling. Some of these are translucent, so you can see a light held near the other side.

Of the less common formations, helictites are among the strangest. They occur on cave ceilings, walls, and floors and appear to have grown in total disregard of the law of gravity. One may start downward, but then turn sideways, upward, over, around, or any way it chooses. It appears to have no reason to it at all. Apparently, the little tube that starts to grow has a center opening so small that gravity does not control the droplet as much as capillary action, hydrostatic pressure, or evaporation. In addition, the calcite crystals are not perfectly symmetrical, and placed one upon another they continuously alter the direction of the tube's growth.

Not all the water that drops to the floor causes stalagmites to grow. If the water flow is fast enough and the drops hit a limestone floor, a small pocket may be hollowed out. If some tiny fragments of material fall into that pocket, they may be agitated by the successive water drops and uniformly coated over their entire surface with minerals brought in by the water supply. The result is round "pearls" that can grow to be 1 inch (2.5 cm.) or more in diameter. There can be a large number of

1. King's Palace, Carlsbad Cavern
2. King's Highway, Carlsbad Cavern

1

2

"cave pearls" in each "nest." Although most pearls are nearly spherical, there can be exceptions. Bat bones have fallen into a nest and become the nucleus for cylindrically shaped pearls.

Recently, geologists have discovered that evaporation and condensation, caused by heat-driven convection within the cave, have strongly influenced the growth and distribution of various speleothems, including the popcorn-like crusts so common in the Big Room. Studies of speleothems in Carlsbad Cavern have contributed much to our knowledge of similar features elsewhere in the world.

There are still more types of formations — lily pads, aragonite trees, gypsum flowers — present in Carlsbad Cavern. We are just beginning to understand how some of them form. To both the scientist and the casual visitor the underground world is proving vastly different from the sunlit surface.

1

2

3

4

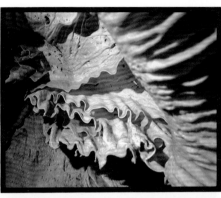

6

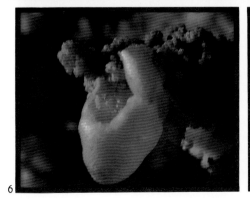

7

1. Epsomite needles frequently grow to 18 inches long but usually break under their own weight. *Ron Kerbo*
2. Draperies, Dome Room
3. Aragonite crystals on soda straw. *Ron Kerbo*
4. A dense cluster of soda straws
5. Close-up of delicate aragonite crystals. *Ron Kerbo*
6. Hydro magnesite balloons. These balloons are very rare and are known to be in only three caves in the United States. *Ron Kerbo*
7. Helictites. Not all the beauty in a cave is large. These helictites have been stained from the water running through iron deposits on its journey downward to the cave. This type of helictite is called "Snake Dancer." *Ron Kerbo*

2

1. Entrance to the Big Room, Carlsbad Cavern. One of the largest underground chambers in the world
2. Papoose Room, Carlsbad Cavern
3. Queen's Chamber draperies, Carlsbad Cavern

3

BY LANTERN'S LIGHT

With the exploration of the cavern and the subsequent establishment of the national park, trails and lighting were provided. The physical shape of the cavern has dictated that the trails be constructed in certain passageways and rooms. Still, the designing of the pathways and the selection of the specific routes have provided the visitor with excellent views of most of the features described here. Although three miles (5 km.) of public trails enable visitors to see much of the cave, a number of other known passageways and chambers exist, which are extremely difficult to reach. Discovery of new areas still occurs on occasion. In 1966 several miles of passageway and several rooms, including the Guadalupe room, were discovered when a park ranger squirmed through a previously unexplored "pinch." In 1982 explorers discovered a room of exceptional beauty and color in a remote section of the cave. The Bifrost Room, named after the Rainbow Bridge of Norse mythology, contains formations ranging from pure white to deep orange and bright red. In 1991 explorers negotiated a series of climbs in the New Mexico Room and discovered over a mile of new passage now called Chocolate High. Explorations continue to broaden our knowledge and understanding of caves. To protect the unspoiled beauty of the new chambers, explorers must wear non-marking boots and establish a single trail for everyone to follow. There are no plans for these areas to be developed or opened to the public because of their inaccessibility.

2

3

1. The Christmas Tree in Slaughter Canyon Cave, Carlsbad Caverns National Park. *Michael Nichols/ Magnum*
2. Cave exploration continues in the park. Not all passages are as large as the Big Room. *Ron Kerbo*
3. Hiking up to Slaughter Canyon Cave

The Guadalupe Mountains are laced with over 200 caves. Within the 46,755 acres (18,896 hectares) of Carlsbad Caverns National Park over 70 have been discovered. Some are small and some are immense. However, no rooms presently known rival Carlsbad Cavern's Big Room in size of 14 acres (6 hectares). There are a number of individual formations in the park's other caves that are larger than anything found in Carlsbad Cavern, and there are certainly many formations that are as spectacular and unusual as any known. Several are pictured in this booklet.

One other cave in the park, Slaughter Canyon Cave, is open to the public on a regular basis. Guided lantern tours are offered through this undeveloped cave by reservation. All the other caves are "wild caves" with no development either accomplished or planned. For safety's sake and for protection of cave resources, permission must be obtained from the superintendent to enter any of these caves. A few are open to recreational caving on a limited basis; others can be entered only in the course of approved scientific research.

Given the wealth of known caves here, one

must wonder how many caverns with no opening to the surface exist in the Guadalupes. What remarkable wonders must exist, unseen, deep in this ancient reef turned desert mountain range.

1. Guadalupe Room, Carlsbad Cavern. Discovered in 1966 when a ranger crawled through a small hole.
2. The Bifrost Room. A recent discovery in Carlsbad Cavern, is one-half mile from the nearest developed trail and requires a rope climb up a 60-foot overhanging wall to gain entry into its chambers. Explorers of this section of the cave must move with extreme caution and forethought to prevent damage to its delicate formations.
3. The Chandelier Ballroom in Lechuguilla Cave, Carlsbad Caverns National Park. *Michael Nichols/ Magnum*

3

IN DARKNESS LIFE...

There are very few creatures on earth that are more misunderstood and shrouded in superstition than bats. Since they fly by night, live in places dark and mysterious and their appearance is somewhat grotesque, stories based on half-truths are accepted as fact.

The early history of Carlsbad Cavern was primarily concerned with the discovery of a large bat colony and the mining of tons of guano. As years pass and research reveals facts about the many species of bats, they must be regarded as one of nature's most unusual and interesting creatures.

The bat is the only true flying mammal — having warm blood, fur, teeth and nursing its young. It is not closely related to either birds or rodents.

Though a large variety of the 50 species of bats found in the United States have been recorded in Carlsbad Cavern, the majority of bats found here are of one species, the Mexican free-tailed, so named because it spends much of its life in Mexico and, unlike most bats, has part of its short tail free from the membrane between its legs. It is small and weighs about ½ ounce (15 gr.) with a wingspread of 11 inches (28 cm.).

The Mexican free-tailed bat is a migratory species, spending summers in the northern part of its range and winters in the more tropical climate to the south. At Carlsbad the colony arrives in April or early May. In recent years the population has numbered about 1,000,000 individuals. At the cavern the bat colony resides in a dimly lit portion of the cave ½ mile (1 km.) from the large natural entrance and near a small rift opening to the surface. The bats hang from the ceiling which is 30 to 80 feet (9-24 m.) above the floor in extremely close bunches. Public trails do not go into this section of Carlsbad Cavern.

In early summer, some caves, including Carlsbad, are nurseries. The young are born shortly after the colony arrives at its summer home. Each mother has one offspring and, surprisingly, at birth the baby weighs about one-fourth the mother's weight. Soon the mother leaves her baby on its own, clinging to the ceiling. Upon her return, a mother lands within a yard of her offspring and finds her baby by its odor and distinct calls.

Learning to fly is an interesting problem for a creature that lives clinging to the ceiling. The first time has to be right: the young bat has to become airborne before it reaches the floor from which it cannot fly and where it will die of starvation.

The bats remain in the dark recesses of the cavern by day, emerging in the evenings to fly all night catching their food on the wing. We do not know what exactly triggers the evening's flight, but it usually begins at sundown. When the bats leave the cave, the denseness of the flight is astounding. At the flight's peak more than 5,000 bats leave the cave each minute.

The physical shape of the cavern entrance causes the bats to rise about 200 feet (60 m.) to reach open space. They fly upward in a counter-clockwise spiral before heading off to find their evening meal.

Bats locate food and navigate by a sound reflection system. Flying with their mouths open they emit a high frequency sound; the sounds bounce back off obstructions, such as flying insects, and the bat's extremely sensitive hearing signals a mental image of what is ahead. Though bats do have eyes and see reasonably well, it has been determined that a bat can be blindfolded and still perform well by this sonar; deprived of hearing or the ability to make sounds, a bat is almost helpless.

The bats emerge from the cave as a group but soon disperse and fly at night as individuals; they cover great distances and do

not land. Their metabolism is high and they require nearly half their own weight in food each evening. It has been estimated that a colony of 1,000,000 bats may consume several tons of insects nightly.

Near dawn they return to the cavern, and the return is as spectacular as the exit. The bats return individually and approach the cave at altitudes from just above the entrance to hundreds of feet in the air. As they circle over the cavern mouth they fold their wings and dive at surprising speeds into the dark hole. In the dive, wind rushing over the thin wing membrane causes an audible vibration; when the return is in full swing, an eerie "buzzing" can be heard.

As summer progresses the babies join the flight. Late summer populations increase several hundred thousand. The colony at Carlsbad Cavern numbered well into the millions before man entered the picture. It is believed that the use of insecticides has been a major cause of the decline of the bats, as they are often poisoned by eating insects which have been exposed to these chemicals. The ban on DDT now in effect in this country should benefit the bat colony.

In late October or November, an evening flight will occur and the colony will not return in the morning. Thus begins their trip to winter quarters in Mexico. Banding at Carlsbad has turned up one bat over 800 miles (1,280 km.) south of the cavern.

People often express fear of bats, generally because of lack of knowledge about them. The danger of vampire bats to man has been greatly exaggerated; they are quite small and feed off livestock and small animals. Vampire bats are not found in the United States except in one or two locations immediately north of the Rio Grande.

The only life native to the dark interior of the cave, other than bats, is several varieties of insect species, most of which are found near where the bats roost. There is little or no food supply for large creatures and there are no running streams within the cave to support fish or salamanders. Since man entered the cave, establishing trails and bringing food, mice and even ringtails have ventured into the cavern to make a home there. However, they are rarely seen and are not native to the deeper portions of the cavern.

The attraction of Carlsbad Cavern is primarily due to the geological wonders found there, but with just a little understanding of life in the darkness, it becomes apparent that in this realm are some of nature's most remarkable creatures.

5

1. A bat flight from Carlsbad Cavern at sunset.
2. 3. & 4. Bat flight from the mouth of the cavern.
5. Mexican free-tailed bat. *Scott Altenbach*

THE PARK EXPERIENCE

Trips into Carlsbad Cavern have been arranged so they can be adjusted to almost any ability or desire. Every visitor first makes the seven-mile (11 km.) drive from the park boundary up Walnut Canyon to the visitor center, located a short distance from the cavern entrance. At the visitor center each person can decide on the trip he would like to take.

The complete cavern tour consists of two parts. The first portion of the trip is a 1¾-mile (2.8 km.) walk through the natural entrance along the trail that drops down the portion of the cave known as the Main Corridor into the scenic rooms. These rooms include the Green Lake Room, the King's Palace, the Queen's Chamber, and the Papoose Room. At the scenic rooms level, the trail has dropped some 830 feet (250 m.) in elevation below the visitor center. From there an 80-foot (24 m.) climb is made up to the 750-foot (225 m.) level and the underground lunchroom where the first part of the tour

ends. Restrooms, box lunches and hot and cold drinks are available here. The visitor should be aware that the first part of the complete tour is somewhat strenuous. Most people in good health can make it easily; however, it can be taxing on persons with health or walking problems.

The second part of the trip is a relatively easy 1¼-mile (2 km.) walk around the circumference of the Big Room. The trail is fairly flat and the most scenic portions can be negotiated by persons in wheelchairs. For those who want to take only the second, and easier, portion of the tour, the elevator from

2

3

1. Hikers, Carlsbad Caverns National Park *Hiram Parent*
2. Bat flight program at natural entrance of cavern
3. Walnut Canyon

the visitor center descends the 750 feet (225 m.) to the underground lunchroom where the Big Room trip begins and ends. All visitors leave the cave by way of these elevators that return them to the visitor center.

A concessioner in the park provides food service and souvenirs along with nursery and kennel service. No lodging or camping facilities are available in the park.

There are several park activities outside of the cavern available to park visitors, such as a half-mile, self-guided nature trail. Park rangers also lead conducted walks during the summer season. The Walnut Canyon Desert Drive is a scenic 9½-mile, one-way, gravel road that begins near the visitor center and loops into the backcountry of upper Walnut Canyon.

In the summer months a bat flight program is given by park rangers at the cavern mouth at sunset, just prior to the time the bats normally fly. An effort is made to schedule the program to allow time for the ranger to tell something about the bats and their life habits and then watch the flight.

Guided lantern tours through undeveloped Slaughter Canyon Cave are given daily in the summer and on weekends during the rest of the year. A visit to Slaughter Canyon Cave is a more rugged and adventurous experience than the walk through Carlsbad Cavern. The trip is somewhat strenuous and should be attempted only by those in good physical condition. The most difficult part is the hike from the parking lot to the cave entrance, in which the trail climbs 500 feet (150 m.) in elevation within a distance of one half mile (.8 km.). Reservations are required to make the Slaughter Canyon Cave trip.

Caves, canyons, mountains, and desert — all are found at Carlsbad Caverns National Park. The opportunity to enjoy them in many ways is available to park visitors.

1. The Underground Lunchroom
2. Entrance to Carlsbad Cavern. *Hiram Parent*
3. The Big Room, Carlsbad Cavern. *Michael Nichols/Magnum*

All photos courtesy National Park Service except where noted.
Edited and coordinated
by Bob Peters and Dan Murphy
Design and production
by Ken Seaverns and Ken Hoagland
Art direction
by Christina Watkins
Printing
by Paragon Press
Salt Lake City, Utah
♻ Printed on Recycled Paper

1. Aragonite encrusted stalactite. *S. Fleming*
2. (fold out) The Big Shot. Taken August 19, 1952, it is the world's largest flash bulb photograph, using 2,400 flash bulbs. The photograph covers an estimated 550,000 square feet. The photographer, E. "Tex" Helm, and his crew spent 16 hours setting up the shot.
3. Balcony, New Mexico Room

Back cover photo. Calcite draperies. *Michael Nichols/Magnum*

CARLSBAD CAVERNS • GUADALUPE MOUNTAINS ASSOCIATION
Carlsbad, New Mexico

ISBN 0-916907-02-0

9 780916 907020